THE INNER POET

Edited By Lynsey Evans

First published in Great Britain in 2024 by:

Young Writers
Remus House
Coltsfoot Drive
Peterborough
PE2 9BF
Telephone: 01733 890066
Website: www.youngwriters.co.uk

All Rights Reserved
Book Design by Ashley Janson
© Copyright Contributors 2023
Softback ISBN 978-1-83565-054-7

Printed and bound in the UK by BookPrintingUK
Website: www.bookprintinguk.com
YB0573Q

FOREWORD

For Young Writers' latest competition This Is Me, we asked primary school pupils to look inside themselves, to think about what makes them unique, and then write a poem about it! They rose to the challenge magnificently and the result is this fantastic collection of poems in a variety of poetic styles.

Here at Young Writers our aim is to encourage creativity in children and to inspire a love of the written word, so it's great to get such an amazing response, with some absolutely fantastic poems. It's important for children to focus on and celebrate themselves and this competition allowed them to write freely and honestly, celebrating what makes them great, expressing their hopes and fears, or simply writing about their favourite things. This Is Me gave them the power of words. The result is a collection of inspirational and moving poems that also showcase their creativity and writing ability.

I'd like to congratulate all the young poets in this anthology, I hope this inspires them to continue with their creative writing.

CONTENTS

Hereford Cathedral Junior School, Hereford

Harry Coleman (8)	1
Milly Clarke (10)	2
Sofia Smith (7)	4
Finlay Webb (10)	5
Charlotte Madge (8)	6
Tommy Facchini Zanini (8)	7
Molly Jones (8)	8
Theo Vargha (8)	9
Theo Fowler (8)	10
Imogen Booton (7)	11
Emilia O'Connor (7)	12
Archie Billig (9)	13
Lorena Andrade (9)	14
Luísa de Almeida Martins (11)	15
Francesca Conlon (9)	16
Seth Allmark (10)	17
Alexander Watkins (8)	18
Henry Vaughn	19
Ava Brady (8)	20
William Morgan (11)	21
Daniel Storey (7)	22
Eva-Mae Powell (8)	23
William Whittal (10)	24
Elsa Crawford (7)	25
Joshua Hodson (8)	26
Cillian Aye-Maung (8)	27
Annabel Beavan (8)	28
George Powell (8)	29
William Milestone (10)	30
Jack Pinnell (8)	31
Henry Billig (7)	32
Sam Lort-Phillips (8)	33
Cheyenne Adams (10)	34
Harriet Baxter (10)	35
Tabitha Batchelor (11)	36
Arthur Chapman (10)	37
Frederick Vaughan (8)	38
Oliver Abrantes Noronha (7)	39
Madeleine Cocozza (8)	40
Molly Parsons (7)	41
Poppy Dorise (10)	42
Finley Wells (8)	43
Ranulf Thomson (8)	44
Summer Baillie (8)	45
Tilly Coleman (10)	46
Jessica Jennings (10)	47

North Petherton Community Primary School, North Petherton

Grace Mantyk (8)	48
Noah Jay (7)	49
Asher Kay (7)	50
Tom Stenning (8)	51
Mariia Vladyka (7)	52
Emilia Virgin (7)	53
Fred Stone (7)	54
Ariana Agere (7)	55
Summer Patterson (7)	56
Rowan Hector (8)	57
Riley Savage (7)	58
Ella Druce (7)	59
Owen Pugh (7)	60
Frankie Foster (7)	61
Charlie Martin (7)	62
Lottie Freer (7)	63
Ezmee Heywood (7)	64
Giselle Heathfield Falcon (7)	65
Asher David Tipney (7)	66

Chloe Fleming (7)	67
David Evans (7)	68
Grace Hetherington (7)	69
Freddie Robins (7)	70
Xavier Hodge (7)	71
Adelina Mazurenko (7)	72
Alesha Burgess (7)	73
Ely Carrillo Wyatt (8)	74
Gracie Bradshaw (7)	75
Adam Biktimir Valetov (7)	76
Emily Whiterod (7)	77
Noah Drew (8)	78
Peyton Priddle (8)	79
Cora Hawkes (7)	80
Oscar Maddock (7)	81
Ethan Woollan	82
Stanley Frost (7)	83
Hendrix Dunn (8)	84
Ivy Carter (7)	85
Henry Hodges (7)	86
Harry Steward (7)	87
Noah Sims (7)	88
Rory McClive (7)	89
Samuel Whiterod (7)	90
Maria Juliane Marques (8)	91

St Bernard's Catholic Primary School, Birmingham

Pippin McTernan (7)	92
Sabah Chand Ibrahimzai (8)	93
Aaryan Ladwa (8)	94
Isa Adnan Malik (8)	95
Minahil Abid (8)	96
Khadejah Khan (7)	97
Suleman Salim (8)	98
Rory Kennedy-Edwards (8)	99
Ismaeel Muhammad Latif (7)	100
Danial Ameen (8)	101
Anaya Naseer (7)	102
Aliza Faisal Khan (8)	103
Ayaan Qasim (7)	104
Maryam Qaderi	105
Zakariya Hashmi (8)	106

Abdullah Farrukh (8)	107
Jeslin Sylvia Arun Jernick (9)	108
Eva Mellerick (8)	109
Abigail Steele (8)	110
Connie Rae Reid (8)	111
Mahrosh Ali (8)	112
Mahnoor Naseem (7)	113
Inayah Zubair (9)	114
Musthafa Ahmed (8)	115
Arafat Hassus (7)	116
Denny Rome (8)	117
Huda Haroon (8)	118
Shehrbano Ammar (8)	119
Laylah-Maryam Arshad (9)	120
Mustafa Qaderi (8)	121
Noah Hargreaves (8)	122
Maleeka Khimji (7)	123
Bismah Ali (7)	124
Ayesha Kennedy (8)	125
Mikail Khalid (7)	126
Yahya Abbas (7)	127
Maxwell Wheeler (8)	128
Ameerah Athaif (7)	129
Emell Rahman (7)	130
Raahim Hussain (7)	131
Jana Fearon Perkins (8)	132
Maysam Khan (8)	133
Jacob Formby (9)	134
Nikhil Ladwa (7)	135
Aimee O'Halloran (8)	136
Oliver Carden (8)	137
Dylan Bullimore (7)	138
Emily Hemming (9)	139
Khalil Shah (8)	140
Yusairah Shofi (7)	141
Faria Anwar (8)	142
Radhika Shah (8)	143
Arham Malik (7)	144
Yousaf Arshad (8)	145
Harry Carden (8)	146
Zainab Aqeel (7)	147
Daniel Ilori (7)	148
Hamna Tahir (8)	149

Sulayman Khurshid (8)	150
Imaan Yasin (8)	151
Sadiya Hassan (8)	152
Owain Read (7)	153
Demir Kivrak (8)	154
Aiza Malik (7)	155
Kal-El Smith (7)	156
Olaf Ostapiuk (8)	157
Neko Carby-Fennel (7)	158

THE POEMS

THE POEMS

I Remember When

I remember when I could sit, eat, draw and watch telly.
I remember when I could play all day.
I could be silly and write a story.
I didn't have to tidy the house or do homework.
I could challenge myself or not challenge myself.
I remember when I could be with my fluffy, old dog, Stanley.
I would have races with my dad.
He would always stop and pretend to be tired so I would win.
I was passionate about writing and I still am.
I used to say, "Mummy, look, I'm as strong as a lion."
I remember when we bought six cucumbers and we would get home with three cucumbers.
Now I'm eight years old and I'm doing the opposite of these things.
I'm doing homework and I hardly have any time to do these fun things.
But boy, I love cucumbers.

Harry Coleman (8)
Hereford Cathedral Junior School, Hereford

My Baking Passion

Hello my name is Milly,
I am 10 years old,
I was born on the 13th,
And it's not unlucky, it's gold!

I love reading and writing,
But my favourite hobby is baking,
I have three siblings,
I know that's a lot but seriously, I'm not faking.

Baking, baking, baking,
That's what I do all day long,

    B eautiful project,
    A mazing experience,
    K ind of not fun tidying up,
    I ncredible tastes,
    N o one is stopping your ideas run wild,
    G enerously shared.

As you can see baking's my thing,
If there's a party a cake I will bring,
My dream is to win under Paul and Prue,
Then open a shop so I can bake for you!

Milly Clarke (10)
Hereford Cathedral Junior School, Hereford

This Is Me!

I like to be myself.
I like to watch Harry Potter.
I like reading, playing netball and basketball, riding my bike, walking the dogs, lego, playing with my sister.
We like to play mermaids and like to gaze at the stars and play board games.
We like to go to our cousin's house and have sleepovers.
I like to play princess and, when the weekend is over, I like to close my eyes and dream of the day at school tomorrow.
Today is school! I love going to school!
When the day is over, I go home and sit by the fire and relax.

Sofia Smith (7)
Hereford Cathedral Junior School, Hereford

This Is Finlay

Funny, adventurous, sporty,
Do I hear you say?
Yes, yes that's me,
And mischievous in a cool sort of way.

Football is my passion
And man of the match is my aim.
As the ball hurtles towards the goal,
I know I am on top of my game.

I love to walk my dog, Lockie,
On adventures we go.
My gecko, Clarkson, would love to join,
But would be far too slow.

But by far the best buzz
Is when I am abseiling
Down a bank on a dry, sunny day.

Finlay Webb (10)
Hereford Cathedral Junior School, Hereford

About Me!

When it is a Monday I am yellow.
I'm always green on a Tuesday and Thursday.
I'm red when my sister takes from me.
I'm blue when I'm ignored.
I'm excited when I'm pink.
I'm orange when I'm tired.
I'm white most days because I'm quiet.
I'm blank when I'm upset.
All of these make a rainbow.
Sometimes
I'm all of them at different times of the day.
Most of my friends would be green on a Thursday and Tuesday.
I love sport and lots of things!

Charlotte Madge (8)
Hereford Cathedral Junior School, Hereford

My Dream World

Welcome to Planet Tommy, where creatures roam around in the scorching sun, and on the country breeze you can hear screaming children jumping into the lake.
On the beach next to the city, you can look up at the pink puffy clouds.
They look like floating marshmallows.
You can hear people screaming at a football match going on.
You can hear the river rushing by you.
You can see the dozing sun as it's almost night.
In the dead of night, you can see cats zooming by.

Tommy Facchini Zanini (8)
Hereford Cathedral Junior School, Hereford

Molly

M y face is blue when I get told what to do.
O h how brown I am when my sister is not a fan of my work, I just stop and think maybe you're pink.
L ying is not my thing and my body goes yellow when I don't do it. I say joy is a good very good thing and it is yellow.
L over of animals my face goes rainbow, not black or brown nor white or grey. Rainbow I do say.
Y es I am a kind of carrot consumer and I am orange, yes I am.

Molly Jones (8)
Hereford Cathedral Junior School, Hereford

Kicking Around

It is a magnificent
Shape. You kick it in the
Goal, it scores for you!
Sometimes yes. It has hexagons all around.
It chips over players and rubs against
The rough, tough grass. Usually, it loves
Being tackled and it just wants to be
Kicked. It hates throw-ins, when it
Does occur it tries to get back on
The field so it just wants to play
Around with everybody but
Sometimes it cheats.

Theo Vargha (8)
Hereford Cathedral Junior School, Hereford

My Dream Earth

My planet Theo would have trees as tall as skyscrapers,
Hills that giggle when you trek up them,
Wind that whistles when it blows,
Rivers longer than continents,
Birds as bright as a rainbow and singing all day,
Animals running all around,
Scenes as alive as the land, beaches as long as countries,
Walks that smile all day,
The snow is deep and powdery with a sun that sings and shines every day.

Theo Fowler (8)
Hereford Cathedral Junior School, Hereford

Imogen's Acrostic Poem

I maginative and creative
M agic is what I like
O ften runs out of ideas
G iggling when I'm with my friends
E nergetic and easygoing
N oisy and I laugh

B usy, lazy and sleepy
O utside a lot
O utstandingly good at working hard
T iny writing
O cean animals are amazing
N obody is as lucky as me.

Imogen Booton (7)
Hereford Cathedral Junior School, Hereford

Me Is Me

E yelashes are long and pretty
M y best friend is Maggie
I am flexible
L ittle dogs are so cute
I am independent
A dventurous and kind

O ften arty
C ourageous
O utside a lot
N ature is me
N ew things every day
O ften blessed with squishy things
R eally funny.

Emilia O'Connor (7)
Hereford Cathedral Junior School, Hereford

This Is Me

My name is Archie
I sit in the corner
Playing the drums
I love football
I love rugby
Fortnite is great
Yep! Yep! Yep!
One of my favourite things to do
Is have a sleepover at my friends
Yes! Yes! Yes!
Are you ready?
I like to sing
My name is Arch
Short for Archie
Very short I am
Short but fast

That's my life.

Archie Billig (9)
Hereford Cathedral Junior School, Hereford

This Is Me

I'm a gamer,
I'm an artist,
I'm kind,
I'm happy,
I'm cool,
I'm smart,
I'm fun,
I'm unique,
And I have a dog,
I have fish,
I have a sister,
I have brothers,
I have friends,
I have an iPad,
I have an Xbox,
I have a great life.

This is me.

Lorena Andrade (9)
Hereford Cathedral Junior School, Hereford

This Is Me

This is me, loves to dance, hates to write
This is me from Portugal not from Spain
This is me, loves to play, hates to work
This is me, loves small dogs, hates big ones
This is me, likes to draw, don't like so much maths
This is me, motivated to do well
This is me, hope to do well in school
This is me!

Luísa de Almeida Martins (11)
Hereford Cathedral Junior School, Hereford

F Is For Me

I'm a festival waiting to come out
I'm as calm as the blue sea
I'm fearless like a lion
I'm as couragous as a cloud
I'm kind and friendly like a bee
I can be big fun
Bang! I'm a shooting firework
I'm a portrait of a cute girl
I think like a playful cat.

Francesca Conlon (9)
Hereford Cathedral Junior School, Hereford

A Cup Of Tea

I can't live without a cup of tea
When I have a cup of tea it warms me
It's like sitting in a hot tub
It's like stepping into a bath
Whenever I drink a cup of tea it makes me want to laugh
Green tea, Yorkshire Tea, I don't really care
Warm tea, cold tea, I could drink it anywhere.

Seth Allmark (10)
Hereford Cathedral Junior School, Hereford

My Colours

I am red when my annoying dad swoops down and takes the remote from me.
I am yellow when I plummet outside with gleeful friends.
I am blue when I fall over, pounding against the floor and I'm wheezing.
I am green when I eat my least favourite vegetables.
I am gold when I do the best things for my team.

Alexander Watkins (8)
Hereford Cathedral Junior School, Hereford

This Is Me

Sometimes I am happy,
Sometimes I am adventurous,
Sometimes I get nervous,
Sometimes I feel low,
Then I look in the mirror and what do I see?
I see me and no one else,
I am unique to me,
I am proud of who I am and how I am,
Always stay true to me, be happy and respect everybody else.

Henry Vaughn
Hereford Cathedral Junior School, Hereford

This Is... Me!

The only one,
The lover of lollipops,
Hockey lover,
The queen of macaroons... yummy,
A chocolate chomper... that's me,
As lovely as a cat,
As playful as a puppy,
Amazing Ava,
Acrobatic Ava,
Kind puppy lover,
As energetic as a kitten,
As sporty as a cheetah,
As funny as a panda,
As fantastic as a flamingo,
This is me!

Ava Brady (8)
Hereford Cathedral Junior School, Hereford

This Is Me

My name is Will, I am small like a bouncy ball
I have got a lot of energy like a firework ready to explode

I am short but fast, my favourite sport is rugby
My favourite food is sushi

I like to mess around, I like to have fun
But my favourite thing is hanging with my mum.

William Morgan (11)
Hereford Cathedral Junior School, Hereford

This Is Me

I like playing rugby and eating roast potatoes.
I like riding my bike when I am playing Sumdog.
I love swimming in the wavey cold sea.
I adore boating while launching Beyblades but I always win.
I love going on James's Gator while watching telly.
I like art and I like doing maths.

Daniel Storey (7)
Hereford Cathedral Junior School, Hereford

Marvellous Me

Hilarious hockey player
Speedy swimmer
Perfect performer.

The oldest one
As playful as a puppy
The queen of ice cream.

As naughty as Matilda
As fast as a cheetah
A stylish singer.

The first one is obviously the best
This is me!

Eva-Mae Powell (8)
Hereford Cathedral Junior School, Hereford

I Hate Poems

I hate poems

H ate poems I do
A poem sucks
T his is me sucks
E very poem sucks

P oems are bad
O nly the best poems suck
E very poem sucks
M ost poems are bad
S illy poems.

William Whittal (10)
Hereford Cathedral Junior School, Hereford

Excellent Elsa

I want to be an athlete,
Doing acrobatics and doing things on hoops,
Designing girls' dresses and being with my sister,
And eating chicken korma,
And gardening in the morning,
And swimming,
I want to find unusual things,
This is me!

Elsa Crawford (7)
Hereford Cathedral Junior School, Hereford

This Is Me

The one that gets away with everything.
The ninja in the house.
The master of macarons and ice cream and everything.
A rich rugby player.
An animal lover.
A speedy swimmer.
A fast runner.
A loud singer.
A funny being.

Joshua Hodson (8)
Hereford Cathedral Junior School, Hereford

This Is Me The Marvellous Me

A crazy karate doer.
The king of katsu curry.
The gorilla fan.
The one with the fantastic brother.
The marvellous little brother.
The ninja in the house.
The god of crocodiles.
As cheeky as a monkey.

Cillian Aye-Maung (8)
Hereford Cathedral Junior School, Hereford

This Is Me!

I am
An animal lover
A sports fan
Enormously energetic (I try not to show it)
A bit of a chatterbox!
Okay, a big chatterbox
The princess of pistachios
A little forgetful
As sporty as a cheetah
A bookworm
This is me.

Annabel Beavan (8)
Hereford Cathedral Junior School, Hereford

It's Me

The bringer of burgers,
A fun footballer,
A forgetful flamingo,
A proud puppy lover,
Ice cream creator,
A funny banana,
A spy dog reader,
A sofa dozer,
A monkey fan.

George Powell (8)
Hereford Cathedral Junior School, Hereford

Rugby

T errible at maths
H appy playing rugby
I love rugby
S porty

I love sport
S aracens

M onster
E xcellent.

William Milestone (10)
Hereford Cathedral Junior School, Hereford

Me, Me, Me!

Fast footballer
Funny friend
Friendly folk
Super speedy
Crazy child
Meatballs master
Youngest one
Guy gamer
As fast as a cheetah
Great guy.

Jack Pinnell (8)
Hereford Cathedral Junior School, Hereford

This Is Me

My favourite activities are football and rugby.
When I grow up I want to be a professional boxer.
I'm a very good fighter and I know how to do my shoelaces.
My brother doesn't.

Henry Billig (7)
Hereford Cathedral Junior School, Hereford

Mind In Me

I am super sporty,
A creative cricketer,
As fast as the wind,
A karate kicker,
A rough rugby player,
A bird lover,
A funny friend,
An animal lover.

Sam Lort-Phillips (8)
Hereford Cathedral Junior School, Hereford

This Is Me

T hankful
H orrifying
I ntelligent
S mart

I ndependent
S mall

M isunderstood
E ager

Cheyenne Adams (10)
Hereford Cathedral Junior School, Hereford

Harriet

H ilarious
A mbitious
R eliable
R emarkable
I maginative
E legant
T errific

Harriet, that is me!

Harriet Baxter (10)
Hereford Cathedral Junior School, Hereford

Tabby

T errifically talented at talking
A nnoyingly awesome
B eautiful at bowling
B reathtakingly big-headed
Y oung and old-souled!

Tabitha Batchelor (11)
Hereford Cathedral Junior School, Hereford

Arthur

- **A** mazing
- **R** ugby
- **T** alented at rugby
- **H** orrible brother (apparently)
- **U** tterly a pet lover
- **R** ugby.

Arthur Chapman (10)
Hereford Cathedral Junior School, Hereford

Animal Explorer

Pokémon fan
Koala lover
The one with the horrible brother
Pony prince
Goat hugger
Good rugby player
Cool runner.

Frederick Vaughan (8)
Hereford Cathedral Junior School, Hereford

This Is Me!

I am good at tennis
I like maths
I like swimming
The bike is fun
I like running to school and home
Playing with my friends is the best.

Oliver Abrantes Noronha (7)
Hereford Cathedral Junior School, Hereford

Marvellous Me

A chocolate chewer
A dog leader
A true lover
Lovely me
Fabulous me
Strong me
Bossy me
Fame seeker.

Madeleine Cocozza (8)
Hereford Cathedral Junior School, Hereford

Molly And The Magic

Summer
Holidays
Sweets
I don't want to tidy my room.
I love water parks.
My dogs are Digby and Barty.

Molly Parsons (7)
Hereford Cathedral Junior School, Hereford

This Is Me!

P uzzled person!
O ptimistic!
P erfect in every way!
P assionate!
Y oung!

Poppy Dorise (10)
Hereford Cathedral Junior School, Hereford

This Is Me

A rough rugby
The little one
Pet lover
Chicken burger eater
Friend
Friend to Sam
This is me.

Finley Wells (8)
Hereford Cathedral Junior School, Hereford

Think

I don't like writing
I would rather think
My teacher told me to think
I think about
Think.

Ranulf Thomson (8)
Hereford Cathedral Junior School, Hereford

Shark Attack

This is a shark.
They have really sharp teeth.
They live in salty water.
They eat lots of fish.

Summer Baillie (8)
Hereford Cathedral Junior School, Hereford

Tilly

T errific
I ncredible
L ovely
L oyal
Y oung.

Tilly Coleman (10)
Hereford Cathedral Junior School, Hereford

This Is Me

J essica
E xcellent in every way
S uper cool
S pecial.

Jessica Jennings (10)
Hereford Cathedral Junior School, Hereford

This Is Me

T ravelling to the beach with animals hugging me in the sea,
H ot tubs are relaxing with a biscuit and a cup of tea,
I love halloumi, oh yes I do, melted cheese and burnt for you,
S eason with a nice restaurant meal.

I am as funny as a clown,
S tomping and clapping of music in the air.

M y family and I like to do the conga,
E lephants and animals, drinking from the sea.

Grace Mantyk (8)
North Petherton Community Primary School, North Petherton

This Is Me

T rapping Pokémon with my fiery volcano
H iding away like a lion ready to pounce
I can see from afar like Pidgeot in the sky
S pying on Squirtle splashing around the poolside

I am as quiet as a mouse
S neaking up behind my Pokémon friends

M y favourite Pokémon is Pikachu, he's tiny but
E veryone knows I play rough.

Noah Jay (7)
North Petherton Community Primary School, North Petherton

This Is Me!

T he food I eat is delicious.
H andwriting is a struggle but it helps me write.
I njuring myself in rugby.
S ummery times on the fields, I play tag with my friends.

I like eating pink bubblegum and sushi.
S wimming lessons I like, and I get certificates when I do it.

M artial arts I like to do, when I punch and kick.
E venings are the best.

Asher Kay (7)
North Petherton Community Primary School, North Petherton

This Is Me

T his is me playing Asphalt 9: Legends on a sofa
H appy houses down my street
I love nuggets more than anything
S inging Christmas carols when it's Christmas

I don't like football, I love football
S illy videos I watch on TV

M y favourite thing to do is play Roblox
E xploring theme parks when I go to them.

Tom Stenning (8)
North Petherton Community Primary School, North Petherton

This Is Me

T he water I play with makes me smile
H andwriting I write makes me happy
I am like a phoenix flying in the sky
S unshine is like a fire phoenix

I like to play Roblox with my friends
S unshine makes me go outside to play

M y favourite food is doughnuts!
E xploring the world outside – it is full of mystery.

Mariia Vladyka (7)
North Petherton Community Primary School, North Petherton

This Is Me!

T rick or treating
H aving a hot dog with my family
I am as sweet as a bee
S chool trips are the best, I love everything, it is the best

I make dinner every night, the lovely tasty smell of the soup
S tockings are hung up, we see the tasty dinner

M e and my brothers playing Luigi and Mario
E nglish is the best.

Emilia Virgin (7)
North Petherton Community Primary School, North Petherton

This Is Me!

T aking on the other players in football.
H eading the ball in the goal.
I love football, it was my dream.
S uccess is helping the goalie not having to save.

I am someone who loves cake.
S o many cakes, cake village.

M y name is Fred and my brother is called Rocco.
E very day amazing fun to play with someone.

Fred Stone (7)
North Petherton Community Primary School, North Petherton

This Is Me!

T rying to be grateful to people,
H igh hopes, delightful dreams,
I n the sea with kind, gentle sea animals,
S inging birds, stop, just listen to how they sing beautifully.

I am happy as a hippo,
S o many zooming cars making noises.

M aking cakes with my sister,
E njoying my life with my family and friends.

Ariana Agere (7)
North Petherton Community Primary School, North Petherton

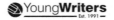

This Is Me!

T he cats are my favourite animal,
H ere at home, my cats are as jolly as elves.
I , myself, as nimble as a cat,
S ummer is my name.

I also love wildcats like leopards, lions, cheetahs and tigers,
S hadow and Jellybean are my two cats' names.

M y cats love me,
E very night they sleep with me.

Summer Patterson (7)
North Petherton Community Primary School, North Petherton

This Is Me!

T remendous snakes, slithering on the floor,
H ow many dogs can we get?
I 've got a dog as fast as a car,
S o many birds in the sky.

I n the goal, left and right,
S o many goals there, flooding the place.

M any buildings in the city,
E very type, we've got them all.

Rowan Hector (8)
North Petherton Community Primary School, North Petherton

This Is Me

T oday I am feeling happy.
H andwriting I like.
I like eating pasta and drinking Tango.
S ummertimes I walk my dog.

I can climb like a monkey.
S ee the sun in the light, sometimes you see it in the dark.

M y dad takes me to Sunday school
E veryone says I am smiley.

Riley Savage (7)
North Petherton Community Primary School, North Petherton

This Is Me!

T he thing I love the most is my sister,
H orses to play with are such fun,
I am as clever as a dolphin,
S o much I have achieved.

I love my precious purple heart gem,
S inging is my hobby.

M y favourite food is cookies,
E ven or odd numbers in maths are my thing.

Ella Druce (7)
North Petherton Community Primary School, North Petherton

This Is Me

T hin chipolatas cooking on the barbecue,
H ot chocolate warming me up,
I ntelligent ice skaters ice skating,
S nakes slithering around.

I gloos as hot as the sun,
S easide waves brushing across my feet.

M onster trucks and motorbikes,
E lephants stomping around.

Owen Pugh (7)
North Petherton Community Primary School, North Petherton

This Is Me

T errifying T-rex on the loose,
H appy like a hyena,
I like reading and enjoying storybooks
S illy billy when I hear jokes.

I want to be an explorer,
S neaky like a slithery snake.

M artial arts fighting club with my friends,
E lephants are my favourite animal.

Frankie Foster (7)
North Petherton Community Primary School, North Petherton

This Is Me!

T ins all greased ready for baking,
H elping people make cakes,
I love eating Rice Krispie cakes,
S aving them for home time.

I n the countryside I love to go on monster trucks.
S loppy, slimy, muddy water.

M onster meditator
E ngines soar across the road.

Charlie Martin (7)
North Petherton Community Primary School, North Petherton

This Is Me

T umbling at gymnastics,
H igh boxing at the gym,
I am as beautiful as a butterfly,
S preading my arms as I am swim.

I am as smart as Einstein,
S melling my baking through the air.

M editating through the breeze,
E njoying my doughnuts whilst watching TV.

Lottie Freer (7)
North Petherton Community Primary School, North Petherton

This Is Me

T umbling at gymnastics.
H arry Potter Land is fun.
I ce cream cones are the best.
S ummer is my best friend.

I n my family, it is fun playing with my baby cousin.
S nakes are my favourite animals.

M um and I like going to the shop.
E zmee is my name.

Ezmee Heywood (7)
North Petherton Community Primary School, North Petherton

This Is Me

T hings I love include cuddles,
H ere at school I love to do music.
I am quiet like a butterfly,
S o much fun with my friends in Spain.

I am kind like a teddy,
S am loves cuddles from Mum.

M y favourite colour is pink,
E very day I love to draw.

Giselle Heathfield Falcon (7)
North Petherton Community Primary School, North Petherton

This Is Me!

T ea and custard creams,
H aving lots of adventures,
I am as fast as the Flash,
S chool trips are fun.

I am as bouncy as a Dalmatian
S lithering through the house, Mars disappears.

M otorcycles make cool noises,
E njoying Harry Potter with Dad.

Asher David Tipney (7)
North Petherton Community Primary School, North Petherton

This Is Me

T rips in my van.
H oliday abroad with my family.
I 'm excited like a monkey.
S wimming in the ocean like a dolphin.

I n the wild looking for creatures.
S chool trips with my friends.

M aking cake in the kitchen.
E ating my cake on the table.

Chloe Fleming (7)
North Petherton Community Primary School, North Petherton

This Is Me!

T aking cakes out of the oven,
H ow sweet cakes are,
I love playing Minecraft,
S illy games are fun.

I love maths, art, English, science and forest school,
S porty and fast, that's me.

M y family is funny,
E ngines revving, wheels zooming.

David Evans (7)
North Petherton Community Primary School, North Petherton

This Is Me

T errific like an amazing person
H appy house you will see
I am as cute as a bunny
S weetly playing with my sisters.

I like being able to do jobs like maths
S isters as kind as friends.

M y favourite lesson is maths
E veryone can be my friend.

Grace Hetherington (7)
North Petherton Community Primary School, North Petherton

This Is Me

T rotting up and down along the road,
H ay and carrots are for my ponies,
I tackle in football to get the ball,
S wimming is fun.

I am as cheeky as a pony,
S chool trips are fun.

M y hobbies are art and music,
E very day I love watching TV.

Freddie Robins (7)
North Petherton Community Primary School, North Petherton

This Is Me!

T rees full of birds,
H ow many animals are there in the world?
I guanas crawling on the floor,
S ea turtles swim through the ocean.

I n a world of football,
S coring in the goal.

M ining a cave in Minecraft,
E xploring the Minecraft world.

Xavier Hodge (7)
North Petherton Community Primary School, North Petherton

This Is Me

T he school is so fun
H andwriting makes me very happy
I like to go to the woods
S nakes are curious like me.

I can run like a cheetah
S un is as happy as me.

M y favourite food is chicken nuggets
E xploring the world is full of mystery.

Adelina Mazurenko (7)
North Petherton Community Primary School, North Petherton

This Is Me

T he teacher is kind,
H elping me with English,
I 'm as clean as my room,
S chool trips are fun.

I am as happy as the sun,
S wimming is my favourite thing to do.

M y cats are faster than me,
E xcited for year four and my new teacher.

Alesha Burgess (7)
North Petherton Community Primary School, North Petherton

This Is Me

T he best game is PK XD.
H ey, I wear glasses.
I 'm as sweet as a cherry.
S anta is as kind as me.

I 'm as cool as epic Ely
S ee my iPad, isn't it nice, I play Roblox every night.

M y favourite food is sushi
E ly is my name.

Ely Carrillo Wyatt (8)
North Petherton Community Primary School, North Petherton

This Is Me

T imes tables are my favourite
H orses are my favourite
I can swim as fast as a dolphin
S miling when I see Mum.

I am as fast as a cheetah
S pending money on toys.

M y favourite toy is red bunny
E lemental the movie is my favourite.

Gracie Bradshaw (7)
North Petherton Community Primary School, North Petherton

This Is Me!

T ight football shoes.
H igh keepy ups.
I n a football pitch meeting buff players
S killful players doing step overs

I n a big stadium like a building
S uper football tactics

M y dream will come true
E very time I score, I celebrate.

Adam Biktimir Valetov (7)
North Petherton Community Primary School, North Petherton

This Is Me

T his is me playing **Roblox** with my friends
H ungry as a hamster
I love chicken nuggets more than anybody
S uper Stitch

I love to be silly
S miley as a monkey

M y favourite things to do are read and play Roblox
E xcellent as an owl.

Emily Whiterod (7)
North Petherton Community Primary School, North Petherton

This Is Me

T ime to ride my bike with my friends
H ugs are the best
I can be a hero
S port is the best sport.

I am hairy as a bear
S crumptious hot dogs are delicious

M arshmallows are my favourite thing to eat
E ating is the best thing ever.

Noah Drew (8)
North Petherton Community Primary School, North Petherton

This Is Me!

T iny poems with giggles,
H appiness spreading all around,
I love doing cartwheels,
S omersaults and jumping jacks.

I love cats and kittens,
S easide holidays at the beach.

M y name is Peyton,
E dith and Holly are my friends.

Peyton Priddle (8)
North Petherton Community Primary School, North Petherton

This Is Me

T omorrow I am going to the fair
H edgehog class is where I am
I am as kind as Mum
S miling when I see Mrs Hill.

I can swim like a fish
S ister Tilly we play Roblox.

M y Tilly texts me pictures
E very day I am smiling.

Cora Hawkes (7)
North Petherton Community Primary School, North Petherton

This Is Me

T aking cakes out of the oven,
H elping Nanny,
I like exploring at forest school,
S neaky as a raccoon.

I like football, taking part,
S coring goals.

M y favourite game is Guess Who?
E very day I like going to school.

Oscar Maddock (7)
North Petherton Community Primary School, North Petherton

This Is Me

T ackling every day, scoring goals
H elping people is my favourite thing to do,
I love dogs
S o many yummy cakes all the time.

I am as cool as a koala
S o much fun doing English.

M y friend is Noah
E than is my name.

Ethan Woollan
North Petherton Community Primary School, North Petherton

This Is Me

T umble to my home
H iya, I say, whilst doing kung fu
I like animals like a zoo keeper
S tanley is my name.

I can run like a cheetah
S tuck in the mud is the game.

M y family is very kind
E lephants are my favourite.

Stanley Frost (7)
North Petherton Community Primary School, North Petherton

This Is Me

T errific bike riding skills.
H alo is my favourite.
I am as sporty as Mr Furs.
S un makes me happy.

I am as strong as a panther.
S port, I like basketball.

M onday mornings, I go for a jog.
E xcited for Halloween.

Hendrix Dunn (8)
North Petherton Community Primary School, North Petherton

This Is Me

T uesday I swim like a fish
H edgehog class is where I am
I am as big as an elephant
S assy like a drama queen.

I can run like a cheetah
S kipping in my garden.

M y mum loves playing with me
E veryone loves me.

Ivy Carter (7)
North Petherton Community Primary School, North Petherton

This Is Me!

T -rex is my favourite.
H appy as a hyena.
I am as brave as an explorer.
S neaky as a serpent.

I am as fast as a racing car.
S illy as a monkey.

M artial arts is what I do best.
E xtreme as a skateboarder.

Henry Hodges (7)
North Petherton Community Primary School, North Petherton

This Is Me

T uesday I swim like a fish
H arry likes Hot Wheels
I am as big as a shark
S miley I am all day

I can swim like a dolphin
S am is my best friend

M y teacher is Miss Curry
E ating doughnuts makes me happy.

Harry Steward (7)
North Petherton Community Primary School, North Petherton

This Is Me!

T ackling on the football pitch,
H aving fun playing in goal,
I score every game,
S triking balls is so fun.

I am called Noah,
S canning for food.

M y friend is Ethan,
E ntertainment is playing football.

Noah Sims (7)
North Petherton Community Primary School, North Petherton

This Is Me

T his is me
H issing when I am angry
I am as strong as a hippo
S illy when we wrestle.

I get scared when we have Nerf wars
S un makes me feel hot.

M onday I go to school
E veryone thinks I am amazing.

Rory McClive (7)
North Petherton Community Primary School, North Petherton

This Is Me

T ravelling around places
H elping tidy away
I can eat as much as a whale
S leepy as a sloth.

I am as fast as a hyena
S mart as a gorilla.

M y favourite thing is food
E xploring the sea.

Samuel Whiterod (7)
North Petherton Community Primary School, North Petherton

This Is Me!

T he new girl at school
H i, I am Maria
I am from Brazil
S peak Portuguese, I am learning English

I love blue
S wimming is great fun

M aria is my name
E very day I go to school.

Maria Juliane Marques (8)
North Petherton Community Primary School, North Petherton

My Dreams

I wish I could go to Australia with my family
I want to swim with the sharks.
I want to see new animals
And explore the rainforest and play in there all day
It is very warm.
This is me!

My hair is as yellow as the sun.
I have eyes as green as grass.
My lips are as pink as a pink dragon fruit.
This is me!

I like my rabbit Willow,
He's like a ball of fur.
He is so cute and he's very nice.
Sometimes he likes to stomp his feet with me.
This is me!

My little brother Daniel says I'm his favourite sister.
He always calls me to play and together we make
a difference.
This is me!

Pippin McTernan (7)
St Bernard's Catholic Primary School, Birmingham

Everything

I can't smell my nose because my nose smells other things.
I can't touch the tip of my finger because the tip of my finger can't touch the tip of my finger.
I can't hear myself snore because I get tired.
I can't taste my tongue because my tongue is in the way.
I can jump, flip and flop all around like a dog.
I don't have a cat because my parents get mad.
I can hop, I can rap, I can be funny all around.
An amazing me can't be perfect all the time.
Mom and Dad are all around.
Super-duper amazed.
You can be perfect like me.
Perfect me.
Enormously smart me.
Rainbow me.

Sabah Chand Ibrahimzai (8)
St Bernard's Catholic Primary School, Birmingham

Me

To make me you need...

To have a birthday on 20th December
Loads of football cards
A sometimes messy bedroom
Like cars and football
Be a Ladwa, have a name called Aaryan Ladwa
Go to Saint Bernard's School
Be a very kind boy
Have friends called Zakariya, Jacob, Ali, Rory and Isa
Eight nearly nine years old

Mix them all together, add some Indian and English, and even McDonald's!
Have love for God!
Add Mr Barnett, Miss McCarron, Mrs Humphreys plus Mrs Brendon!
Reading as well!
Last but not least, just me!

This is me!

Aaryan Ladwa (8)
St Bernard's Catholic Primary School, Birmingham

My Favourite Game

My favourite game,
You definitely play it, obviously,
It was popular when it came out,
But, sadly, not now,
You earn beans and the worst colour is red,
You can sabotage and kill,
You can vote, and throw out,
You do tasks in weird maps
There are different roles like:
Engineer – you can fix things and invent
Crewmate – the least favourite in most countries,
Imposter – not really the best,
Shape-shifter – oh, now we're talking,
And now the finale of my favourite game is:
You fool, did you think I was going to stop there?

Isa Adnan Malik (8)
St Bernard's Catholic Primary School, Birmingham

I Am Minahil

I like the colour purple as cool as a pool.

A flamingo is as cute as a newborn cat.
M e and my cousin Ayat are the best of friends.

M ila and Ruqaya are as kind as nurses.
I like art because I love drawing, especially designs.
N obody is as smart as me because I know what 100 + 100 is.
A nts are so cute especially when they walk.
H orses are so kind when I ride.
I love my family, they help me so much and they are so sweet.
L ollies and pizza and mac n cheese and fries.

Minahil Abid (8)
St Bernard's Catholic Primary School, Birmingham

Riding Bikes

Riding bikes, I love to do it so much,
I love Just Dance 2021 so much,
Doing funny dances makes me laugh so much,
I went to the windmill to get my bird nest,
Nest, inside is a baby bird,
Green I hate, but blue I like.
Bike, I love to ride to the park,
I love my family so much,
Could you be kind like me?
Rumaysa is my sister,
In science, we make pretend volcanos,
I love my cousin's babies so much,
Lovely is what I am
On my reading table, we have the panda's kippers,
End of the day prayer,
Sister.

Khadejah Khan (7)
St Bernard's Catholic Primary School, Birmingham

My Hobbies

T o go out into nature is so much fun, I see plants and
H elp the plants. It is so fun to do it in the sun.
I love football, it's my hobby, I've got lots of hobbies.
S ometimes I lose, sometimes I win and it doesn't matter because I don't even score goals.

I like being a chatterbox, me and my friends do it a lot.
S ometimes it is funny, sometimes it is not.

M e and my family, I love them, my younger sister's name is
E va, my older sister's name is Ayat.

Suleman Salim (8)
St Bernard's Catholic Primary School, Birmingham

How To Make Me

This is what you need to make me:
A house full of toys
Ten iPads
Liverpool football players
A sprinkle of friendship
A slice of happiness
A book of school
A country full of food
Miss McCarron

Now this is what you need to do:

Fry a slice of happiness then add a book of school and mix.
Then add Liverpool football players and five iPads to the mix.
Finally, add half the toys and cook.
For the last thing sprinkle the friends, the rest of the toys,
And Miss McCarron.
That is how to make me!

Rory Kennedy-Edwards (8)
St Bernard's Catholic Primary School, Birmingham

I Am Unique!

My passion is classic cars,
I like Arctic blue,
I am helpful and compassionate,
I stand up for everyone and anyone,
My hair is black like darkness,
My eyes are brown like hazel and chocolate,
I can run fast like a cheetah,
I am unique!
This is me!
Football is entertaining and fantastic,
Formula One racing is thrilling and really enjoyable,
I love fruit, especially cucumber,
I look forward to holidays, particularly those in faraway lands,
I am unique!
This is me!

Ismaeel Muhammad Latif (7)
St Bernard's Catholic Primary School, Birmingham

Danial The Rapper

Generous, kind, super-fast mind.
Maths is my superpower but I don't like English.
But I like maths and makes me a sporty fan.
I like Ronaldo not Messi
even though he won the World Cup.
Ronaldo is the goat, Messie is the shark
and when I am in a bad mood, a super quick end
and I go to matches whenever I can go.
There's a line like my hairline, ahh, I am a rapper.
The end like you think.
I am gonna give up now, actually the end,
Psych, got you again, the rapper gone.

Danial Ameen (8)
St Bernard's Catholic Primary School, Birmingham

I Am Unique!

I like pink
I have brown hair like a chocolate bear
I have brown eyes
I am kind
This is me!

Christmas
It is the best time of year
You can spend time with family
It makes me happy
It is so much fun
Snow and snowflakes are so much fun
This is me!

Dreams
I wish I could fly like a bird or an angel.

Birthday
You get presents, cake and you get older.

Eid!
You pray, have fun and eat.
This is me!

Anaya Naseer (7)
St Bernard's Catholic Primary School, Birmingham

I Am A Chatterbox

I am a chatterbox you know what I mean.
I'm a fast-paced little girl you know.
I chat you know but you know I love everything, this is me!
This is me you know who I am.
I am an awesome little chatterbox you know what I mean.
I am also a little diva you know what I mean.
I love being a little diva but my favourite hobby is being a little chatterbox and that's me you know.
I chat wherever I am, I never stop chatting,
I never stop batting and that is me!

Aliza Faisal Khan (8)
St Bernard's Catholic Primary School, Birmingham

The Best Catcher

I am fast, I can save.
I am a fast-paced goalie.
I can save your goals and I can kick the ball far.
When Liverpool loses I feel sad.
When I tell people my favourite team is Liverpool, they say that Liverpool are the worst.
That makes me feel mad.
I play football, I get better and better.
Until I win I'll bet my friend who is 10 years old when I will achieve this goal
I will be wriggling about.

Ayaan Qasim (7)
St Bernard's Catholic Primary School, Birmingham

Who Is That?

M ysterious and unlikely to bump into you that you might find it funny
A ttached to Maltesers and M&M's
R emember to bring your favourite friends Faria, Maysam, Bliss and Imaan
Y ummy Maltesers did you know she can smell them from a mile away?
A rt, sketching, drawing and painting that is what she likes best
M agnificently fast and happy you can find her at school. It is me!

Maryam Qaderi
St Bernard's Catholic Primary School, Birmingham

Zak Can Rap!

My name is Zak and I can rap.
I like to play ball in my house hall.
I am eight and was born in Belgium.
I am kind, caring and obedient.
Big fan of football, watching Man City winning the treble while my mum is heating the kettle.
There is nothing I need except a slice of pizza but how could I forget my fav Italian pasta?
I have a good habit of helping others so you can always count on me.
This is me!

Zakariya Hashmi (8)
St Bernard's Catholic Primary School, Birmingham

My Favourite Things

My favourite holiday is going to Scotland and Pakistan.
My favourite food is apples and pancakes.
My favourite transport is a car.
My favourite sport is cricket.
My favourite colours are red, green, orange, yellow, and maroon.
My favourite player is Babar Azam and Ronaldo.
My favourite song is 'Black Route'.
My favourite games are 'Brookhaven and Paradis Islands RP', and Livetopia.

Abdullah Farrukh (8)
St Bernard's Catholic Primary School, Birmingham

How To Make Me

To create me you will need,
A book full of love,
A hot cheesy pasta,
A pinch of fastness,
Lots of fun,
Lots of reading,
A sprinkle of brightness.

Now you need to,
Add a book full of love and hot cheesy pasta, lots of fun, a pinch of fastness,
Mix it with a sprinkle of brightness,
A few minutes later, add lots of reading,
Then leave it to cool down,
This is me!

Jeslin Sylvia Arun Jernick (9)
St Bernard's Catholic Primary School, Birmingham

The Rap About Me

My name is Eva and I like to play, even though I am a little shy
I like to dance with my friends, but sometimes my friends are a little silly

I love to have a little bit of fun
And my dream time job is to be a dancer or a singer
I do love food, but if I eat a lot I might get sick.
If I get a job, I will be a billionaire

So that is my life if you want to know.
So, yeah!

Eva Mellerick (8)
St Bernard's Catholic Primary School, Birmingham

My Favourite Things

I love my family because they hug, they cuddle,
And even sometimes snuggle.
I like happy friends, it makes me smile
But after a while I need to say bye.
My hair is brownish gold,
It isn't very cold.
I love reading, it is my favourite thing,
When I'm hungry I sometimes wish it was a sweet.
My cousins are far away, I wish they could stay in England so we can play games.

Abigail Steele (8)
St Bernard's Catholic Primary School, Birmingham

Why I'm Perfect?

I am perfect, I can cook but I can't clean,
You don't see me in a washing machine,
I'm perfect, sensible and cool,
I'm no fool,
You see me, I'm an appalling person,
I'm a star but I'm not that perfect,
People see me and they get nervous because they think I'm horrific, but I like to eat biscuits,
I'm amazing, you're hallucinating.

Connie Rae Reid (8)
St Bernard's Catholic Primary School, Birmingham

My Acrostic Poem

M y name is Mahrosh. I am kind to everyone.
A ll I really love is my mum. She is funny!
H ere is what my favourite thing is: melons.
R ain is not my thing in the winter. Summer is my thing.
O h, there are still some more things I want to tell you.
S pooking people is what I do.
H ere, it's done. I hope you enjoyed my poem.

Mahrosh Ali (8)
St Bernard's Catholic Primary School, Birmingham

I Like... But

I like yellow but I don't like pineapple.
I like playing basketball but not football.
I like the sunset but not drawing it.
I like running to the park not driving.
I like koalas and pandas but not snakes.
I like to run but not to walk.
I like games but not jokes.
I like nature but not rain.
I like grass but not bugs.
I like dancing but not singing.

Mahnoor Naseem (7)
St Bernard's Catholic Primary School, Birmingham

Who Is This?

Who is this person I find fascinating?
Is he an actor, or is he a fish?
He's handsome and romantic,
A good actor and has three kids.
Who is this person I like?
Is he a billionaire, or is he a trillionaire?
Is he famous or is he rich?
People call him SRK.
Oh no, that's a big hint!
Have you figured it out?
It's Shah Rukh Khan!

Inayah Zubair (9)
St Bernard's Catholic Primary School, Birmingham

My Favourite Stuff

B eing good is great as a mood, I like food.
R ods are to catch fish to eat its meat.
O n Monday we eat lovely food.
T o key stage two, they pay for food.
H ere is a packed lunch and it has good food.
E nd of lunch break, we did maths and I passed.
R est of school, we've got no rules and chilled in a good mood.

Musthafa Ahmed (8)
St Bernard's Catholic Primary School, Birmingham

Making A Difference

Making a difference is the best ever, even small things make a huge difference.
Like giving to charity, recycling and much more.
Making a difference is the best ever, you can make a very big difference by smiling, picking up litter and walking instead of driving.
Being generous is good, like sharing, helping and more.
Nature is good, it has green and muddy colours.

Arafat Hassus (7)
St Bernard's Catholic Primary School, Birmingham

A Recipe To Make Me

You will need:
Games
Pizza
Tea
Peas
Potatoes
Sports
Television

Mix together a lot of games, and with those games a lot of pizza,
Add some peas and potatoes (I love potatoes!)
Stir in lots of tea,
Mix in some sports, since I'm sporty and fast,
Finally, add lots of television, and that is how you will make me!

Denny Rome (8)
St Bernard's Catholic Primary School, Birmingham

This Is Who I Am!

I am kind,
I have a mind,
I am intelligent,
I love tennis,
I love singing,
I love dancing,
I like colouring,
Same as drawing,
I like baking,
I love cats,
I like bats,
I like pink,
I like chicks,
My favourite friends are Sabah and Anaya Fatima.
I am beautiful,
I am helpful,
This is who I am!

Huda Haroon (8)
St Bernard's Catholic Primary School, Birmingham

About Me Rap

So I like soup
How much I like to lose?
Every time I lose, everyone boos,
How I like to rule,
Really I like to rhyme,
But I like to be fair,
Anyway, I have lots to rhyme so keep listening to hear my lines,
No way, I am almost done I better hurry this up,
Oh, this is my last line, bye, have a nice life.

Shehrbano Ammar (8)
St Bernard's Catholic Primary School, Birmingham

This Is Me!

T ennis is my favourite sport.
H istory mainly cools my brain.
I ce cream is a mini fan to me.
S ome call me Einstein.

I love to read all the time.
S weets are my easy treat.

M ilk is the drink I love.
E ggs are the breakfast thing I adore.

Laylah-Maryam Arshad (9)
St Bernard's Catholic Primary School, Birmingham

To Make Me

To make me...
You need my friends and my family.
You need football and Ronaldo cards.
Add some Mbappé and Ronaldino shirts.
Throw in some Real Madrid posters.
Some days at school.
That is me!
Ha! Ha! Just kidding.
I love reading and maths.
I love sports.
That is me now!

Mustafa Qaderi (8)
St Bernard's Catholic Primary School, Birmingham

My Rap

I'm as smart as Einstein.
I'm as fast as The Flash.
I'm small as a pea
but kind like a tree.
I'm generous with a quick mind.
My friends are always on my side.
Sometimes I can be very quiet like a mouse.
Sometimes I can be loud like a lion.
I am me...
That is a fact!

Noah Hargreaves (8)
St Bernard's Catholic Primary School, Birmingham

Stewardship Of Creation Is Lovely

Nature is beautiful, more beautiful than a bright star,
It is the best on a sunny day, looking at a jug of flowers,
I could look at flowers for hours, they are the best,
Flowers are the best, I could gaze at them all day,
Grass is so green and so clean, like an apple, I love grass,
Nature is the best!

Maleeka Khimji (7)
St Bernard's Catholic Primary School, Birmingham

I Want It – Give It To Me Now

I want this toy – give it to me now.
I want this cake – give it to me now.
I want this ice cream – give it to me now.
I want that book – give it to me now.
I want that cupcake – give it to me now.
I want that sharpener – give it to me now.
Sharing is hard!

Bismah Ali (7)
St Bernard's Catholic Primary School, Birmingham

My Imagination

Koala bears are my favourite thing
They are cute, they stand out
They are grey and snuggly.
Nature is green
Nature is one
Nature makes me happy
Nature makes me think of me
Art is anything
Anything at all
Art is messy and fun
Arty things make me... well, me!

Ayesha Kennedy (8)
St Bernard's Catholic Primary School, Birmingham

This Is Who I Am

I am a boy
I am kind
I have a mind
I am smart
I am friendly
I like football
I have a tent
I like blue
I am bright
I have a watch
I like rats
I am brave
I am strong
I like my brothers
I like cricket
I am good
I like swimming.

Mikail Khalid (7)
St Bernard's Catholic Primary School, Birmingham

The Caribou Cup

I went somewhere
To watch the football.
I played table tennis while the match was on.
When it was half-time,
I played driving games.
The grown-ups were in another room,
So my cousins and I played in another place.
Before I left, I watched Dad play a football game.

Yahya Abbas (7)
St Bernard's Catholic Primary School, Birmingham

Superstar Striker

S uperstar striker playing football,
P atiently waiting for the ball,
O ccasionally getting the ball and doing his fancy dribbling,
R unning with the ball with his new boots,
T ightly squeezing past defenders,
S coring loads of goals!

Maxwell Wheeler (8)
St Bernard's Catholic Primary School, Birmingham

I Am A Masterpiece!

I am unique
I am bold
I can stand up for myself
I love helping people
I am a great friend
I want to make a difference, but together we are a masterpiece!
We can be a masterpiece together
We could make a difference together and this is the best I can be!

Ameerah Athaif (7)
St Bernard's Catholic Primary School, Birmingham

A Red Big Heart

When I go into the hall to sing hymns
My heart goes
Bright like a hot volcano,
So bright in the sky.
Why does my heart glow when I,
Hear Mrs Ezekiel
Play the beautiful piano,
And it makes my heart glow,
Like a diamond in the sky.

Emell Rahman (7)
St Bernard's Catholic Primary School, Birmingham

Raahim

R ead this poem, it's the best.
A t school, I play with my friends.
A waterfall pours a lot of water.
H igh mountain tops.
I eat my favourite fruit, strawberry.
M ountains are tall, you can climb them.

Raahim Hussain (7)
St Bernard's Catholic Primary School, Birmingham

Who Am I?

What is fearless but filled with happiness?
Has two best friends.
Violent when endangered.
Brave when she needs to be.
Has nightmares about demons.
Her dad is a retired professional boxer.

Can you guess?

It's me!

Jana Fearon Perkins (8)
St Bernard's Catholic Primary School, Birmingham

Favourite Animal

A paw as gentle as a cloud,
And the sound of a whisker,
Fur as soft as silk,
With sparkling shiny eyes,
As calm as a sunset,
Pretty as a flower,
Gentle as a summer.

Can you guess the animal?

Answer: A cat

Maysam Khan (8)
St Bernard's Catholic Primary School, Birmingham

Guess The Animal

I am green but with some spots,
I also like to hop on lots of pots,
I eat flies with my really long tongue,
When I'm a baby, I can't go on land,
If you touch me you will die,
What am I?

Answer: A poison dart frog.

Jacob Formby (9)
St Bernard's Catholic Primary School, Birmingham

I Like Animals

I like dogs, cats and hamsters.
I have fun playing with those animals.
They are fluffy and cute.
My heart goes bright red with fun when I play with them.
My hands feel nice when I stroke their fluffy-fluff.
I feed them dark brown food.

Nikhil Ladwa (7)
St Bernard's Catholic Primary School, Birmingham

The Crazy In Me

A wonderful child,
A wandering mind,
And always kind.
A pizza menace,
An animal lover,
And a super fast runner.
A habit for sports,
And last, but not least, a crazy child,
So that is all about me, so...
Bye bye!

Aimee O'Halloran (8)
St Bernard's Catholic Primary School, Birmingham

Marvellous Countries, A Riddle

The flag has a dark ash colour with a bit of red and white
People admire the country
Tourists love the country
The country has lots of mysteries
The capital of the country is Cairo.
Where is it?

Answer: Egypt.

Oliver Carden (8)
St Bernard's Catholic Primary School, Birmingham

I Am Dylan

I like swimming

A pples are nice to eat
M um is a superhero

D ad is fun
Y ou are funny...
L awson is my friend
A pps are great
N o one is as clever as me!

Dylan Bullimore (7)
St Bernard's Catholic Primary School, Birmingham

You Can Make Me By Adding

A cup full of drama,
A bucket full of giggles,
A loving companion,
A tidy bedroom,
A heap of happiness,
Five teaspoons of brightness,
Add a whole lot of love and friendship
Plus a pinch of creation and imagination.

Emily Hemming (9)
St Bernard's Catholic Primary School, Birmingham

My Recipe...

To create me, you will need:
Sweets,
Ice cream,
Weetabix and Coco Pops,
Nacho cheese,
A football,
Messi,
Minecraft and Fortnite,
Roblox.

Mix it all.
Sprinkle some fun.
You made me!

Khalil Shah (8)
St Bernard's Catholic Primary School, Birmingham

Me And The Dashing Cat

I have a cat, she is so nice and sweet,
I always hug my cat,
She eats food with me,
She loves me very much and I do too,
She is a very smart cat,
She comes to me when I am sad,
She is like a sister to me.

Yusairah Shofi (7)
St Bernard's Catholic Primary School, Birmingham

Faria Is Me!

F un with friends!
A mazing with fun!
R esponsible with any challenge!
I maan, Maryam, Maysam and Bliss are my BFFs!
A ll the time, you will see me with my friends and family!

Faria Anwar (8)
St Bernard's Catholic Primary School, Birmingham

Who Is This?

Beautiful eyes,
Long lovely hair
Loves to eat pizza,
Loves tigers and elephants and safari animals,
Loves lovely cinnamon Cheerios,
Birthday is in October,
Who is this?

This is me!

Radhika Shah (8)
St Bernard's Catholic Primary School, Birmingham

I Am A Footballer

I am a kind footballer,
I am a kind helper,
I am a defender,
I am a good defender,
I block the ball,
I am a good runner with the ball on the pitch,
I am a football watcher,
This is me.

Arham Malik (7)
St Bernard's Catholic Primary School, Birmingham

All About Me

Y o-yos are my favourite toy
O ranges are my favourite fruit
U nique in my own way
S weet like sugar is my personality
A nd my favourite sport is
F ootball.

Yousaf Arshad (8)
St Bernard's Catholic Primary School, Birmingham

Me Recipe!

A recipe to make me...

Sporty
Fast
A bit of tea
Toast
Video games
Virtual reality
A third comic book

Stir it all in,
Put it in the oven,
That's me!

Harry Carden (8)
St Bernard's Catholic Primary School, Birmingham

My Birthday Party

I was excited because it was my birthday,
Everyone was coming over and I was so happy,
And we were going to eat chocolate cake,
After, when everyone went home,
I said goodbye, and then they went.

Zainab Aqeel (7)
St Bernard's Catholic Primary School, Birmingham

Feelings

Angry because I don't like not studying interesting subjects.
Lonely when I have no friends,
Happy because I love watching cartoons,
Awesome because I run fast like a cheetah chasing its prey.

Daniel Ilori (7)
St Bernard's Catholic Primary School, Birmingham

My Mystery Animal

I have brown spots around me.
I am part of the big cat family.
My home is the jungle.
I am as fast as a cheetah and as violent as a tiger.
What am I?

Answer: Leopard. (inverted)

Hamna Tahir (8)
St Bernard's Catholic Primary School, Birmingham

Sulayman

S ensible
U sually plays football
L oves cats
A mazing
Y ou will like me
M arvellous
A musing
N ever gives up.

Sulayman Khurshid (8)
St Bernard's Catholic Primary School, Birmingham

This Is Me

I ntelligent in school
M agnificent at trying to complete everything
A mazing at trying my best
A wesome
N ever gives up.

Imaan Yasin (8)
St Bernard's Catholic Primary School, Birmingham

My Life

I love playing with my friends.
I love playing with my dad too.
He taught me how to ride a bike.
He takes me everywhere with him.
That is me.

Sadiya Hassan (8)
St Bernard's Catholic Primary School, Birmingham

I Am Not A Human, I Am So Good At Football

I like football.
I am like Haaland.
I can strike before you can blink,
So you better watch out for me,
Because I can see you when you sleep.

Owain Read (7)
St Bernard's Catholic Primary School, Birmingham

This Is Meeeeee!

I like chocolate
I can do anything for you
I like maths
I like my mum
I like sweets
I like books
I like reading.

Demir Kivrak (8)
St Bernard's Catholic Primary School, Birmingham

I Love Reading

Reading is so fun
I like to read in the sun.
The more you read
The more you learn.
Reading is so fun.
This is me.

Aiza Malik (7)
St Bernard's Catholic Primary School, Birmingham

Kal-El

K ind
A pples are juicy
L oving my mum and dad
E ating wraps
L ike to play football.

Kal-El Smith (7)
St Bernard's Catholic Primary School, Birmingham

Jump Out!

My name is Olaf,
I like hot Cheetos,
Rugby is the best,
Fifty feet in the air,
Jumping out of a helicopter.

Olaf Ostapiuk (8)
St Bernard's Catholic Primary School, Birmingham

Neko

N ike shoes.
E ating spaghetti.
K ittens to stroke.
O ranges are juicy.

Neko Carby-Fennel (7)
St Bernard's Catholic Primary School, Birmingham

YOUNG WRITERS INFORMATION

We hope you have enjoyed reading this book – and that you will continue to in the coming years.

If you're the parent or family member of an enthusiastic poet or story writer, do visit our website **www.youngwriters.co.uk/subscribe** and sign up to receive news, competitions, writing challenges and tips, activities and much, much more! There's lots to keep budding writers motivated!

If you would like to order further copies of this book, or any of our other titles, then please give us a call or order via your online account.

Young Writers
Remus House
Coltsfoot Drive
Peterborough
PE2 9BF
(01733) 890066
info@youngwriters.co.uk

Join in the conversation!
Tips, news, giveaways and much more!

 YoungWritersUK   YoungWritersCW   youngwriterscw

Scan me to watch the This Is Me video!